KINGFISHER KNOWLEDGE

INVENTIONS

KINGFISHER
KNOWLEDGE

INVENTIONS

James Robinson

Foreword by
James Dyson

KINGFISHER

BOSTON

Senior editors: Simon Holland, Hannah Wilson
Coordinating editor: Stephanie Pliakas
Senior designer: Peter Clayman
Picture research manager: Cee Weston-Baker
Picture researcher: Rachael Swann
Senior production controller: Lindsey Scott
DTP manager: Nicky Studdart
DTP operator: Claire Cessford
Indexer: Carron Brown

KINGFISHER
a Houghton Mifflin Company imprint
222 Berkeley Street
Boston, Massachusetts 02116
www.houghtonmifflinbooks.com

First published in 2006
10 9 8 7 6 5 4 3 2 1
1TR/0606/TWP/MA(MA)/130ENSOMA/F

LIBRARY OF CONGRESS CATALOGING-IN-PUBLICATION DATA
Robinson, James.
Inventions/James Robinson.
p. cm.—(Kingfisher knowledge)
Includes index.
ISBN-13: 978-0-7534-5973-7
ISBN-10: 0-7534-5973-6
1. Inventions—Juvenile literature. I. Title. II. Series.
T48.L44 2006
600—dc22
2005031660

ISBN-13: 978-0-7534-5973-7
ISBN-10: 0-7534-5973-6

Printed in Singapore

GO FURTHER ...
INFORMATION PANEL KEY:

Web sites and further reading

career paths

places to visit

Contents

A collection of turbines harnessing energy from the wind close to Palm Springs, California

Foreword

At school you are taught English, math, and science, but I imagine that few of you have had the good fortune to attend a lesson in invention. If invention classes were taught in school, they would, I think, be very popular. Just imagine . . . "In today's lesson we are going to learn how to invent the robot that will do all your homework. Next week we will be creating the contraption that will transport you from your home to school with a snap of a finger." It's the stuff of science fiction!

As it stands, invention is shrouded in mystery. Perhaps you've heard the story of Archimedes, an ancient Greek mathematician who had a flash of inspiration and solved a long-pondered problem while taking a bath. Famously, he cried, "Eureka!" (which means "I have found it!") and ran, stark-naked, through the streets. As a child I was told this legendary tale of scientific discovery—and a magical story it is too! The problem, though, is that it makes invention seem just like . . . magic. And unless you're Harry Potter, magic is not something that you can easily learn at school. Fortunately, however, for most engineers and scientists, invention is much more a case of experimentation, of trial and error. Sure, there are occasional sparks of genius, but mostly a new invention comes down to a curious mind, determination, and creativity—things that you all have.

Whether you are interested in the invention of airplanes, robots, nanotechnology, or even vacuum cleaners, the starting point is always frustration and problems. In the case of airplanes, for example, why are we earthbound in our transportation? Why can't we copy the elegance, speed, and freedom of, say, birds? Why can't we fly? In my case, I started by asking questions such as "Why do vacuum cleaners fail to do the job for which they were designed?" and "Why do they lose suction?"

From frustration, the next step is figuring out the cause of the problem. Here, I recommend a hands-on approach—taking things apart! When I was faced with the problem of the offending vacuum cleaner, I decided to cut it open and find out exactly what was causing the problem. So, where next? Well, it's at this point that a so-called "eureka" moment can come in handy. You need an idea. My idea was to do away with the vacuum cleaner bag and replace it with a cyclone, which proved to be a much better way of sucking up dust.

But an inkling of an idea is just the starting point. Trial and error is the key to transforming the spark into a reality. My first, very crude, prototype was simply made from cardboard and gaffer tape attached to the body of my old vacuum cleaner. This was the first step in a long process of developing my invention. There were 5,126 more prototypes before my invention was complete. So think about this the next time you call a friend on a cell phone, listen to music on your shiny new MP3 player, or ride in a car. While these inventions do amazing things with apparent ease, behind each one there are people, like me, taking things apart, testing things out, trying something new, having fun. Why don't you try it too?

James Dyson

James Dyson, design engineer and inventor of the cyclone vacuum cleaner, the Sea Truck Boat, and the Evolutionary Ballbarrow

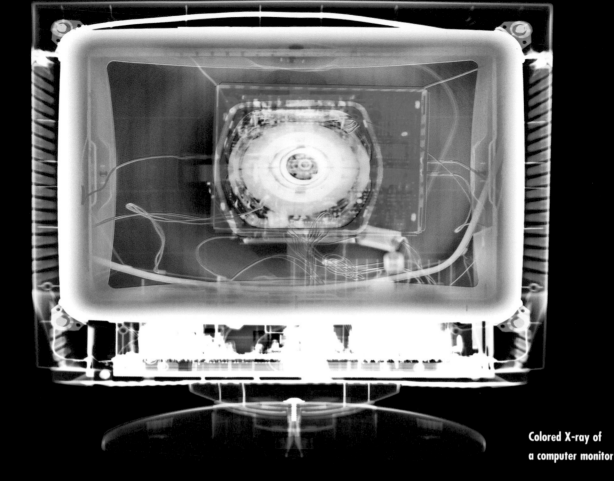

Colored X-ray of
a computer monitor

CHAPTER 1

Communication

We live in a chatty, noisy world of communication. We cannot do anything without exchanging words, radio signals, or data. Our homes and offices are filled with telephones, fax machines, and computers with e-mail. And our pockets jangle with cell phones and keys that send out tiny radio messages to open car doors. Yet 100 years ago, communication meant the tapping of Morse code, the smudgy ink of newspapers, or the scratch of a pen. A torrent of clever inventions changed all that. Communication became popular— and then essential—to our lives. Today we keep information moving on a global web of wires and waves. Communication satellites soar above us, and, beneath our feet, optical fibers glow with data, carrying information faster than the blink of an eye. Even when we get tired of talking, e-mailing, and text messaging, it is the communication industry that entertains us, as we tune in to movies, television, and radio stations.

The telephone

A musical ring from your pocket. Maybe it is the call that you have been waiting for? You hit the talk button—"Hi!" Making calls while on the move or sending a text message—even to another country— is so easy that we take it for granted. It is no longer unusual to watch a movie on a phone or to pick up an e-mail from one. Until 1978, however, technology was not advanced enough even to make a cell phone call around the corner—let alone around the world. Earlier phones all trailed a cable, linking them to the tangle of wires that connected calls.

▲ Early telephones, like this "candlestick" model from 1913, had a separate mouthpiece and earpiece and no dial. Callers spoke into the microphone on the top of the stick and listened through the earpiece. Dialing numbers was impossible—instead people spoke to an operator, who connected calls by pushing plugs into the correct sockets at a telephone exchange.

Telegraphy

Amazingly, this network of wires came before telephones themselves. The wires buzzed not with voices, but with "Morse code"—an alphabet of short and long electric pulses. This method of sending messages was called telegraphy. The first person to send a voice along a telegraph wire was Italian-American Antonio Meucci (1808–1896). His lack of English and his poverty stopped him from developing his invention. Scottish-American teacher Alexander Graham Bell (1847–1922) created the first practical telephone system in 1876.

The first cell phones

By the 1950s, undersea cables linked telephones around the world, but in other ways phones hardly changed until the invention of cellular (cell) phones around 30 years ago. The first handsets were the size of bricks. They beamed calls to antennae on nearby phone masts, which were linked to regular telephone lines. Each antenna provided calls to one "cell" (a small area of good reception), so the new phones were called cell phones. By 1991, cheaper, tinier computer chips made possible the digital cell phones that we use today.

▼ Today's cell phones are small and compact, with built-in aerials. Many of them also act as cameras and allow us to send photographs across the airwaves.

▲ A cell phone can be a useful piece of safety equipment, because if you are lost or injured, you can call for help. But remember—often there is no reception in remote regions. Many people live in areas that are so remote that telephone wires have never reached them. Cell phones may at last take calls to these distant corners of the world, as building just one tall antenna to serve a whole village is cheaper than running telephone wires to every single house.

The future of phones

In wealthier, well-connected countries, phones keep getting cheaper, smaller, and more stylish. Picture and movie calls are already common, and tomorrow's phones will perform the same functions as small computers. Linked to the Internet, they will let you control your home from far away. You will be able to program your TV, turn on the heating, and let out your cat— all from your handset. Maybe you will even use it to make calls too!

Fiber optics

Inside a glowing glass thread, 10,000 telephone conversations buzz. These threads of glass, each the thickness of a human hair, are called optical fibers. Lying on the seabed, they relay phone calls and data between continents. On city streets, they bring hundreds of TV channels into homes. Fiber optics, which is the transmission of information through optical fibers, works by guiding beams of light. "Smart" electronics crams data into each glowing beam. Reflected from the fiber's shiny walls, the beam travels many miles without losing strength.

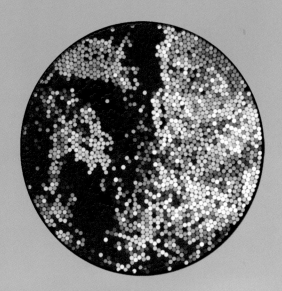

▲ Inside a fiber-optic communication cable there is a bundle of optical fibers. In this picture, which is six times larger than actual size, the dark circles are fibers that are out of use and aren't carrying data.

Bouncing light

Compared to the copper wires they replace, fiber optics is cheaper, more reliable, and carries more information faster. Fiber optics has these remarkable qualities because each fiber has a perfectly clear core. A very shiny cladding (wrapping) gives the fiber a mirrorlike coating. Light shining in at one end bounces along endlessly, no matter how the fiber is bent or twisted. To send information down a fiber, computers first turn it into a digital form—a string of on-off signals. These power a laser at the end of the fiber, flashing the beam quickly on and off. Circuits at the other end change the pulsing light back into an electric current.

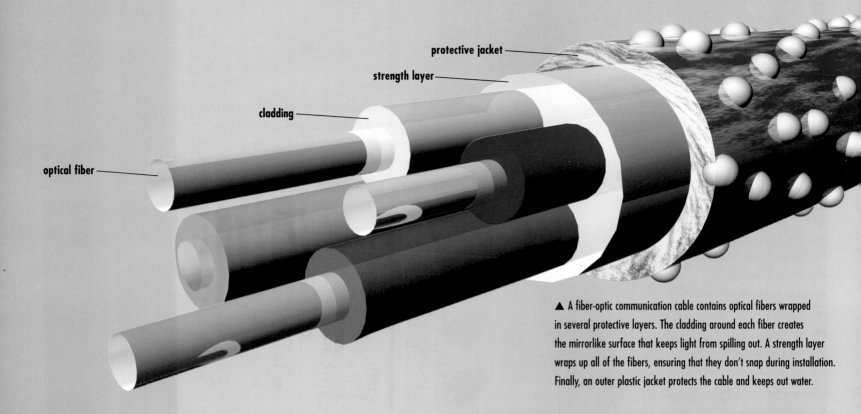

protective jacket

strength layer

cladding

optical fiber

▲ A fiber-optic communication cable contains optical fibers wrapped in several protective layers. The cladding around each fiber creates the mirrorlike surface that keeps light from spilling out. A strength layer wraps up all of the fibers, ensuring that they don't snap during installation. Finally, an outer plastic jacket protects the cable and keeps out water.

Illuminating water

Fiber optics did not start as a way of sending messages, and the first experiments used water, not glass threads. In 1870 British physicist John Tyndall (1820–1893) showed that by lighting up a jar of water, he could make the light run along a curving jet of water flowing from a hole in the jar. In other words, he discovered that the jet of water acted like a mirror, reflecting light within the flowing stream. Fiber optics lit up aircraft cockpit dials from the 1920s, but the first fiber-optic communication cable was not laid until 1977.

The many uses of fiber optics

Today most fiber optics is used in communication, but it does many other jobs too. In hospitals, a bundle of fibers with a lens at each end is called an endoscope. This device allows surgeons to peer inside a patient's body. Extra fibers carry a beam of light to brighten the darkness inside the lungs or internal organs. The fibers' bendability lets them turn the tightest of the body's corners. Engineers use similar devices to look inside sewer pipes or parts of aircraft that are normally hidden from view.

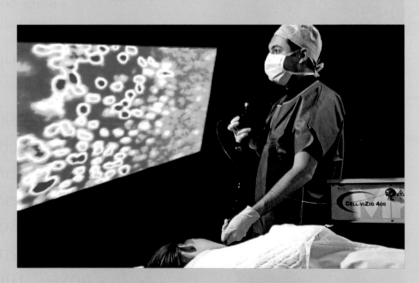

▲ Using optical fibers, doctors can put a microscope inside the human body. They guide a probe, just one third the size of a human hair, toward diseased tissues. Then the "Cellvizio" device displays greatly magnified images from the probe onto a computer screen.

Communication satellites

The next time you are outside just after dusk or before dawn on a clear, dark night, look up. You may see a tiny pinprick of light moving quickly across the sky. It is not a star. It is not an aircraft. It is a satellite, circling Earth thousands of miles above your head. Satellites play a major role in communication. They provide us with television channels, phone calls, and Internet connections. Satellites do other jobs too. Some watch the weather or the stars, guide travelers, or act as "spies in the sky."

◄ This weather satellite is observing a hurricane on Earth. Like most communication satellites today, it is "geostationary" because it appears to hover motionlessly above Earth. The satellites that you see moving across the night sky circle Earth much more quickly and are in lower orbits.

▲ This photograph, taken in 1962, shows technicians in New York testing the *Telstar* satellite a few days before it was launched into space. *Telstar* was the first communication satellite, and it carried TV images and phone calls across the Atlantic Ocean between the U.S. and Europe.

Geostationary satellites

These satellites were the idea of English science-fiction writer Arthur C. Clarke (born 1917). Geostationary satellites appear to be stationary (not moving) because they orbit (travel around) Earth at the same speed as it rotates. The rotation of Earth takes exactly one day, and the satellites also take 24 hours to complete their orbit. In 1945, when space exploration was impossible, Clarke suggested that such satellites might provide a cheap, worldwide television system. Clarke's dream came true less than 20 years later. The first geostationary satellite, *Syncom 2*, was launched in 1963. It broadcast TV to one half of the world.

▼ The first communication satellites used radio telescopes, like this one in Hawaii, as receiving dishes. Today many dishes are less than 3 ft. (1m) wide.

The ups and downs of satellite signals

Communication satellites work like a game of "telephone." They receive microwave signals broadcast from an uplink station on one side of Earth. Then they "pass them on" to a downlink station on the other side of the planet. Uplink and downlink stations are not always far apart. Satellite TV is often broadcast from an uplink station (usually a big satellite dish) in the same country as the TV viewers. The downlink stations are the small dishes on their houses.

Satellite navigation

Today we rely on satellites for many things besides TV. A Global Positioning System (GPS) uses 24 low-orbit satellites to broadcast navigation signals. Sailors, pilots, drivers, and hikers use the signals to find out where they are. "Looking satellites" have discovered new galaxies, and they have helped prove beyond a doubt that Earth's climate is warming. Earth observation satellites can be "spy in the sky" satellites, spotting hidden weapons of war or detecting farmers who cut down protected forests.

▼ This photographer, working in the foothills of Mount Everest, is using a portable satellite receiver dish to exchange conversations and pictures with his colleagues in London, England. For conversations only, satellite phones not much bigger than normal cell phones can be used.

Computers

How many computers do you use each day? If you think it is only one or two, think again. It is more likely to be at least a dozen. The computer you use to do your homework, send e-mail, or surf the Internet is just the start. Smart, fast computers run your cell phone, and if you withdraw money from an ATM machine, you are using a whole network of connected computers. Even your toaster or washing machine probably has a computer chip inside. Without computers, our familiar, comfortable world would grind to a halt.

Mechanical computers

The first computers whirred and clunked with brass gear wheels. They were the invention of English math genius Charles Babbage (1792–1871). Babbage's machines were tricky to build, however, and computers did not succeed until electronic parts replaced moving parts. The first device that you might recognize as a computer was built in around 1940 by Bulgarian-American scientist John Atanasoff (1903–1995). Like today's machines, it worked digitally, using a "binary" system that stored and added numbers as a series of on-off (one-zero) electric pulses.

▲ To create the microprocessors that power modern computers, engineers etch a pattern of tiny components onto a silicon chip using a photographic process. This microprocessor is small enough to fit on an adult's thumbnail, yet it contains 1.35 billion transistors. It's 1,000 times more powerful than the room-sized Colossus computer (right), which was built 50 years earlier.

▲ This is Colossus, the first electronic digital computer. It was developed by the British in 1943, during World War II, to try to translate coded messages by the Germans. Like all early computers, *Colossus* was huge and heavy, and, according to the magazine *Popular Mechanics,* this wasn't going to change—in 1949 the magazine reported that "Computers in the future may weigh no more than 1.5 tons."

Size matters

In the late 1950s, computers began to get smaller as hot glass valves were replaced by transistors—devices that control an electrical current. The integrated circuit, invented in around 1960, squeezed hundreds (later millions) of transistors onto a single tiny chip. This helped computers shrink to the size of a refrigerator by the mid-1960s. The first home computers, which appeared around ten years later, were around the same size as modern home or office computers. Today we are obsessed with size and portability—laptops are not much bigger than a sheet of notebook paper, and your cell phone is a sophisticated computer that can fit in the palm of your hand.

Quantum computers

Although today's computers still perform calculations with the binary system, this could soon change. Quantum computers use the properties of the tiniest particles to add, subtract, and store numbers. Defying common sense, these small particles can be in several places at once, so each one can store many numbers. Quantum computers are very difficult to build, but they will be faster and more powerful than any machine that we use today.

▲ Cheap and tiny, computer chips can now even control and guide toys. These Aquaroid swimming robots, launched in Japan in 2000, use computer guidance to mimic the behavior of real fish.

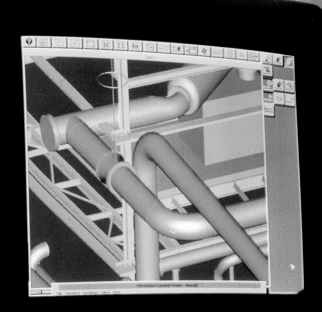

▼ An architect uses CAD (computer-aided design) software to plan the construction of an oil refinery.

The Internet

It spans every country in the world; 500 million people use it each week; it doubles in size every year. The Internet is vast, valuable, and spreading, but what exactly is it? It's a way of connecting computers and a set of rules to control how they talk to each other. Devised in the United States in the 1950s as a way to launch nuclear weapons, the Internet left behind its warlike past long ago. Today we use it to download music, sell things, and keep in touch with friends.

▲ Programmer and computer scientist Tim Berners-Lee dreamed of an easy-to-use program that would let him find and read many different types of data, no matter where and how it was stored on the Internet. Berners-Lee's first words-only Web browser achieved this, but the Web got very popular only when later browsers, such as Mosaic, made it possible to add pictures.

The birth of the World Wide Web

In 1989 English computer programmer Tim Berners-Lee (born 1955) was working on an international science project in France and Switzerland. He figured out a simple but clever way to link information. Inside pages of text on a computer screen, he hid special codes. The codes highlighted words, showing that they were linked to other pages. Clicking on the words changed the page, displaying the new, linked text. Berners-Lee called his code hypertext markup language (HTML) and the pages that used it the World Wide Web.

SAMSUN

◄ Today people all over the world use the Internet without ever really thinking about what it is or where it is. The Web makes this possible, linking together billions of pages of information on millions of computers. The Internet existed as a network of connected computers in the 1980s, but, until the invention of the Web, only scientists and computer experts could use it.

The arrival of e-mail

The Web made the Internet simple to use, and as more and more people got connected, they discovered another fantastic idea—e-mail. Computer expert Ray Tomlinson (born 1941) devised e-mail in 1971. He chose the "@" ("at") symbol to separate a computer user's own name from the name of the network that connected him or her to the Internet. Together, e-mail and the Web made the Internet an extraordinary success. By 1993, Internet use was almost doubling each month.

Googling

As the Web grew bigger, finding information became harder. Search engines attempted to solve this problem. These software robots follow links between pages and make a searchable index from the words on each page. The most successful of all search engines, Google, does much more than this. It judges the importance of each page it finds by counting the pages that link to it. Today, Google is so popular that it has become a verb: "Don't give me the Web address—I'll just Google it."

▼ The Google search engine began as a research project at America's Stanford University in 1996 by inventors Sergey Brin (born 1973) and Larry Page (born 1973). It is named after a "googol"— the number ten multiplied by itself 100 times.

Radio

Turn on a DAB (digital) radio, and you'll hear stereo sound without the hiss and crackle that can spoil traditional radio reception. DAB is short for "digital audio broadcasting," the technology that makes this possible. DAB uses computer processing to turn sound into a stream of zeroes and ones that arrive at your radio exactly as they were broadcast. A computer inside a DAB radio turns the digital signal back into music or speech—and can even show song titles, sports scores, or station information on a display screen.

▲ Introduced in 1954, transistor radios were small and light enough to carry around, for "go-anywhere" music. They are still just as popular.

Radio stations

Radio as we now know it began on Christmas Eve 1906, when Canadian inventor Reginald Fessenden (1866–1932) broadcast speech and music for the first time. Hardly anyone heard it, however, because radio receivers were still rare and expensive. Popular broadcasts did not begin until 1920, when the radio station KDKA went on the air in the city of Pittsburgh, Pennsylvania. Only two years later, there were 600 American radio stations. More than one million people tuned in to their broadcasts.

▲ The first radio signals were broadcast in 1894 by Italian student Guglielmo Marconi (1874–1937). His crude transmitter could broadcast only a Morse-code alphabet of short and long crackles. At the time, messages in Morse code were sent along telegraph wires (see page 8), and so Marconi called his invention "wireless telegraphy."

▲ Pocket-size and no bigger than a deck of cards, this DAB radio has a built-in MP3 player and recorder (see page 35). There are buttons to record live radio programs and to pause them. A standard-sized cable plugs into the socket on the side for downloading music from a computer.

Entertainment

We are still tuning in to the radio. Despite competition from TV, CDs, and other types of entertainment, radio is very popular. Why? Because countless radio stations provide us with a huge variety of free programs. And because radios work almost anywhere. Some are small enough to fit behind our ears—others can be wound up, for music without batteries.

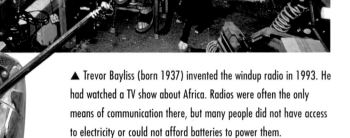

▶ A windup radio is powered by a handle that, when turned, coils up a spring. As the spring slowly unwinds, the radio plays. Solar panels often provide backup power.

solar panels

crank handle

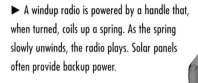

▲ Trevor Bayliss (born 1937) invented the windup radio in 1993. He had watched a TV show about Africa. Radios were often the only means of communication there, but many people did not have access to electricity or could not afford batteries to power them.

A powerful way to communicate

Since its earliest days, radio has been used to hold one-on-one conversations across the world or just around the corner. Taxi drivers and police forces use radio communication because it allows a constant and direct link between two stations—and once the hardware (equipment) has been bought, radio use is free. Today low-power transmitters and computers make radio even more useful than ever before. Radio waves connect computers to printers, scan the bar codes on your groceries, open doors, and make life easier in millions of other ways.

▲ The armed forces communicate by radio because they often operate in areas in which cell-phone antennae or telephone lines do not exist or have been destroyed. Military radios include powerful software that translates conversations into code, preventing information from getting into the wrong hands.

Television

Not long ago, watching TV meant wiggling an antenna on top of the set and choosing from only three or four channels. Today most of us enjoy flicker-free pictures and stereo sound and may be able to choose from hundreds of channels beamed to us from a satellite. Tomorrow's TVs promise better pictures and even more choice—once they are wired to the Internet, we'll be able to throw away the TV guide and watch what we want, when we want.

▲ In 1926 inventor John Logie Baird showed that TV was possible. TV broadcasts began soon after, but only around 30 people watched them— on homemade sets. The pictures were blurred, flickering, and silent. When regular TV broadcasts began, Baird's spinning-disk system was forgotten.

▼ The first TV shows were broadcast live, just like plays. In the U.S. shows often featured the sponsor's name or product. As the giant tube suggests, toothpaste paid for this 1951 quiz show, "Strike it Rich."

The arrival of the television

Scotsman John Logie Baird (1888–1946) was the first person to make a working television, though his spinning-disk system produced small, crude pictures. An electronic system invented separately in the U.S. by Philo Farnsworth (1906–1971) and Vladimir Zworkin (1889–1982) led to the TV sets that we use today. Early pictures were in black-and-white; color TV broadcasts did not begin until the 1950s.

▲ Look closely at a TV screen— you'll see that it's made from thousands of tiny, colored dots.

Live studio audiences

All early TV was "live"—viewers watched programs at the same time as they were happening in a studio. It wasn't possible to record TV programs until 1953. The first video recorders were vast machines that used almost a mile of tape for every 100 seconds of programming. Video cassette recorders (VCRs) appeared in the 1970s, and today's digital video disc (DVD) players began to replace them 20 years later.

Channel hopping

Television is a big part of our lives; most of us watch it for four hours each day—more time than we spend reading, playing sports, or meeting friends, all put together. Fortunately, TV is getting better. Digital broadcasting already squeezes many more TV programs into the limited number of channels available. New TV sets are all digital too; they include smart computers that put supersharp, wide-format images up on their flat screens.

▼ Future TV screens may be flexible, wafer-thin, cheap—and printed using ink-jets. Light-emitting polymers (plastics) glow when electricity passes through them. Printed in a grid pattern, they can display moving TV pictures.

▲ Cable and satellite television stations broadcast hundreds of channels. Advertising pays for many of them; viewers pay to receive many more. Some of the channels appeal to special groups of people such as fans of game shows or people who like to fish. These special-interest channels can thrive because new technology has dramatically cut the cost of running a TV channel.

Going digital

The switch to digital TV also improves the way that you control your TV—it will become much easier to choose programs, watch sports from different angles, buy things, or vote in on-screen competitions. And because digital TV channels are just computer data, TV stations can be broadcast over the Internet. Very soon, downloads could replace your local video rental store; you will be able to watch almost every movie you have ever heard of—but you will still have to pay for them.

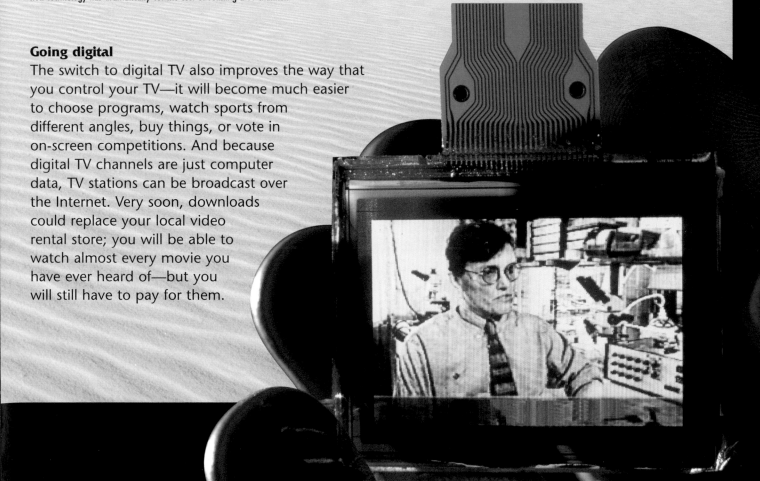

Movies and cinema

On a movie screen, heroes turn into hideous monsters, astronauts fight wars in space, and dinosaurs come to life to chase terrified scientists. Cinema's special effects look so real that it is hard to believe that computers created them. Computers can turn a few extras into a vast army and can change a city studio set into an Arctic ice floe or a tropical jungle. But filmmaking was not quite so easy before the arrival of computer animation.

▲ Optical toys, such as this zoetrope from 1834, showed moving pictures before the invention of cinema or even photography. Small drawings, each slightly different, were placed around the inside of a metal drum. By spinning the drum and looking through the slits in the side, the viewer saw the pictures one after the other. Each blurred into the next so that they seemed to move.

Early cinema

In the earliest movies, the novelty of a picture moving on a screen was itself so astonishing that special effects were hardly necessary. The first movie, shown in 1894 by English inventor William Dickson (1860–1935) and his American employer, Thomas Edison (1847–1931), simply featured a barber's shop and a blacksmith, among other subjects. The audience members paid five cents each to watch the 20-second-long movie in a "kinetoscope," which is a device that creates the illusion of moving pictures.

▼ The jaw-dropping "pod racer" scenes from *Star Wars: The Phantom Menace* use computer animation to take the viewer on a dizzying low-altitude flight. When the *Star Wars* series began in 1977, computers were too slow to create such realistic animation effects.

Sound and color

All early movies were silent and shot in black-and-white. When the actors spoke, their words appeared in writing on the screen. Movies with sound—or "talkies," as they were known—were not really practical until around 1925. Color came sooner to the cinema. There were crude color movies by 1906, but 50 years would pass before even one half of all movies were made in color.

Animation

Artists began making animated movies (cartoons) in 1906. To make their creations come to life, they drew hundreds of similar pictures, with moving objects positioned slightly differently in each one. Photographed and projected in rapid succession, the images danced into action. Computer animation uses a similar method. Animators create a movie frame by frame. They no longer laboriously draw each picture, however. Instead, they build electronic "models" of everything that moves. Wrapping the models in realistic textures and lighting them in a lifelike way complete the movie illusion.

◄ ▲ Cute cartoon characters begin their lives on animators' computers in the form of colored meshes called "wire frames." They do not look lifelike, but they are quick and easy to make. Turning them into believable figures, such as Mike Wazowski from *Monsters Inc.*, takes longer than the wire-frame animation—this movie took more than four years to complete.

▼ Watching a 3-D (three-dimensional) movie, the audience reaches out to touch objects that seem to be right in front of them. Special glasses make sure that viewers' eyes see two slightly different pictures. Their brains merge the images to create the illusion of depth.

SUMMARY OF CHAPTER 1: COMMUNICATION

Phones to satellites

The cell phones that make our lives so easy have been around only since the 1970s. Regular telephones began 100 years earlier, sending voice messages along wires designed to carry the clicks of Morse code. Modern phone calls still travel along copper wires. Over longer distances, speech and data are more likely to travel as bursts of light on fiber-optic cables. International calls also use a network of communication satellites. Like radio stations in orbit around Earth's equator, these satellites relay calls between dishes on opposite sides of the globe; they carry TV images as well.

Computers getting connected

Modern communication relies on computers. Although mechanical computers existed

A geostationary satellite studies a hurricane on Earth

in the 1800s, programmable electronic computers began only around 50 years ago. Integrated circuits, invented in the 1960s, made computers small and cheap enough to put on every desk. The Internet that linked them together was once a military network for controlling missiles. In the 1990s, it expanded rapidly with the invention of e-mail and the World Wide Web—an easy-to-use, point-and-click interface.

Digital broadcasts

Computers and digital technology power our entertainment, too. Digital broadcasts squeeze many more channels into the limited number of radio and TV wavelengths available. Even movies rely on computers—for animation and special effects and, increasingly, for every part of their production, from the cameras to the screen. However, movies, radio, and TV have histories that are much longer than that of the computer—movies began as moving pictures in 1894; radio first crackled into life around ten years later; and pictures flickered on the first television screens in 1926.

Go further . . .

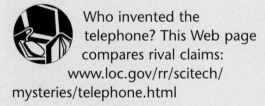

Who invented the telephone? This Web page compares rival claims:
www.loc.gov/rr/scitech/mysteries/telephone.html

Build your own Web site and learn how the Internet works:
www.webmonkey.com/webmonkey/kids/lessons/index.html

"Marconi calling" is a busy site about the inventor of radio communication:
www.marconicalling.com

Communication: From Hieroglyphs to Hyperlinks
by Richard Platt (Kingfisher, 2004)

Satellite Fever by Mike Painter (Ashgate Publishing, 1997)

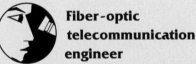

Fiber-optic telecommunication engineer
Lays and repairs fiber-optic cables and installs equipment linking them to a communication network.

Satellite controller
Keeps satellites operating normally, checking and installing software and monitoring their performance.

Application software engineer
Writes software to create programs for computer work (not for systems).

Radio broadcast assistant
Helps with the day-to-day running of a radio station by researching radio programs, dealing with guests, and handling listener feedback.

Find out about the history of television, movies, and digital media at:
Museum of the Moving Image
35 Avenue at 36 Street
Astoria, NY 11106
Phone: (718) 784-0077
www.movingimage.us/site/site.php

Learn all about the telephone at:
The Telephone Museum
McConnell Drive, Wolverton
Milton Keynes MK12 5EL, U.K.
www.mkheritage.co.uk/TTM

Explore vintage computers at:
Computer History Museum
1401 N. Shoreline Boulevard
Mountain View, CA 94043
Phone: (650) 810-1010
www.computerhistory.org

CHAPTER 2

Technology in the home

Surging through the wires that are found throughout our houses, electricity is like an invisible—but essential—servant. It lights and heats the rooms, it keeps our food fresh in the fridge, and it takes the hard work out of unpleasant chores. Electricity powers many other household inventions that stop us from feeling bored or lonely, and it runs the smart and ever-smaller devices that we use to record and remember our lives.

Channeled around the chips of a digital camera, battery power records crystal-clear photographic images. In a camcorder, these electric pictures spring into action, forming a video diary of special moments that we want to cherish forever. And in video games and portable music players, it is electric power that makes racing cars roar and songs soar. So, the next time you flip a switch, spare a thought for Thomas Edison, the inventive genius who, with his creation of the lightbulb, first brought electricity into the home around 125 years ago.

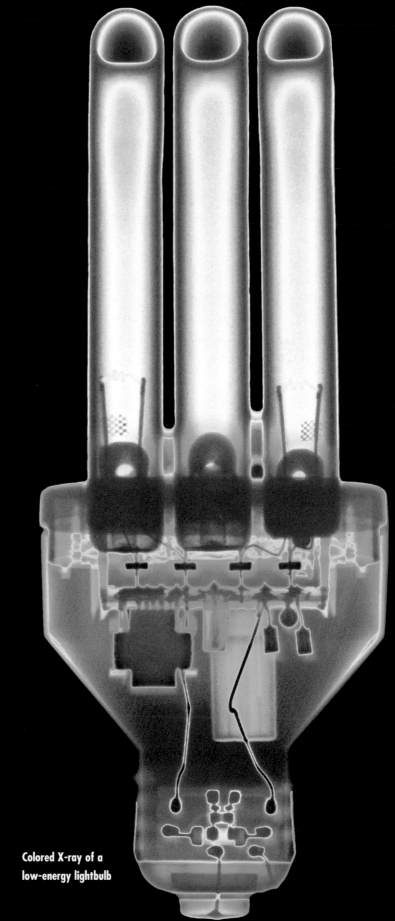

Colored X-ray of a low-energy lightbulb

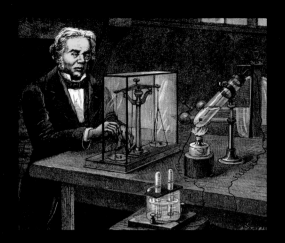

◄ Nobody invented electricity. It is a natural form of energy that was not fully understood until the 1800s. Though many scientists studied electricity and helped us use it, Michael Faraday (1791–1867) did more than most. He was the first person to show how movement and magnetism could, together, produce electricity. He made the first dynamo (electricity generator) and the first electric motor.

Electricity and light

Flick a switch, and a light comes on. It is an everyday miracle that we take for granted—until there is a blackout. Then, we are in the dark. Without electricity, we cannot heat or clean our homes, cook our food, or watch TV. Blackouts remind us that there is much more to electricity than lightbulbs and appliances. Each switch connects us to a vast grid of thick cables and a network of power plants.

The first lightbulb

Thomas Edison was only one of many inventors who tried to create the lightbulb. He succeeded in 1879, using a glass bulb that had been emptied of air. The glowing filament inside was made from sewing thread, baked to turn it into black carbon. Edison's bulbs were the first electrical appliances. They replaced flickering candles and gas lamps—but only in homes that were connected to electricity supply cables. Edison's company laid cables in the streets and built power plants—his lightbulbs would have been useless without a power supply to make them glow.

▶ At night, these shops in Shanghai, China, are brought to to life by electricity.

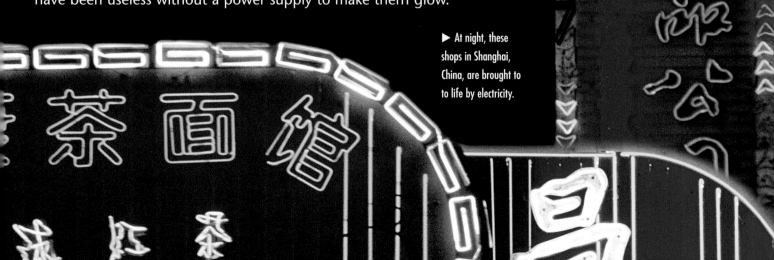

Power plants

Today all developed countries rely on networks of thick cables to carry electricity from power plants to homes, factories, and offices. Most power plants generate electricity from fossil fuels—coal, oil, or gas. Burning these fuels turns water into steam, which spins huge turbines. These in turn power the dynamos that create electricity.

▲ A satellite view of Earth at night shows who has the power. A pattern of light picks out cities in Europe, North America, and south and east Asia. Africa is mostly in darkness. This is because fewer people live there, and those who do cannot afford electricity.

Renewable energy

Saving electricity is important because Earth is running out of the coal, oil, and gas that we burn in order to create it. And when we burn these fossil fuels, harmful gases are released, which trap heat in our atmosphere. This changes the climate and destroys wildlife. It is also melting the world's glaciers, which could raise sea levels and drown our cities. To stop this from happening, we must use less power and harness new sources of energy such as wind, water, and the Sun.

▶ Wind turbines, such as these, generate power without using up scarce resources. They do not produce the exhaust gases that trap heat in the atmosphere. Electricity produced without burning fossil fuels is called renewable energy. We can produce it not only from wind but also from tides and water dams. Though renewable energy can help stop climate change, we cannot produce enough of it to replace fossil fuels. We must also use less power.

For many years after the invention of photography, cameras were huge and hard to use. They needed tripods (three-legged stands) to keep them still. This 1877 image shows a park photographer who developed pictures in his handy darkroom cart.

By the late 1900s, cameras were small, light, and easy to use. Single-lens reflex cameras, such as this one, had interchangeable lenses so that photographers could magnify distant details—or take pictures in a room as small as a telephone booth.

Photography

How can you capture a memory and keep it forever? With a digital camera, it is easy. These compact electronic gadgets are always there when you need them because they are small enough to slip in your pocket. And when you have frozen a moment that you never want to forget, you can look at it immediately on an LCD (liquid-crystal display). Or you can connect the camera to a computer to print or e-mail your photo or post it on the Web.

The first captured images
Photography was very different when it was invented in 1839 by Frenchman Louis Daguerre (1787–1851). The cameras he used were huge and heavy. Taking each picture took 20 minutes—so he could not record moving subjects. Making the picture visible required dangerous chemicals and a darkened room. The pictures, called daguerrotypes, looked more like mirrors than prints. Photography gradually got easier. Cameras got smaller and could soon capture moving subjects. With Kodak's introduction of cheap, simple "box cameras" in 1900, anyone could take pictures.

Digital chips

It was computer chips that made digital photography possible, removing the film and chemicals. Today's digital cameras use dozens of chips. At a camera's heart is a chip that is sensitive to light. Working like digital film, this chip records the image projected onto it from the camera's lens, turning light into computer data. More chips process the data. They use it to show the image on the camera's LCD. Finally, they store it on yet another chip inside the camera's memory card.

▲ X-rays are a form of invisible radiation. Their high energy allows them to pass through solid objects that block light. Captured on film, X-rays can produce a photograph of broken bones—or cracks in pipes.

▲ Connected to a digital camera by a simple cable, a laptop computer can display every picture you have taken today—or fill the screen with a single colorful image.

▼ With digital cameras, it is easier to take clearer pictures, but smart cameras cannot replace photographic skills—especially when attempting tricky, high-speed shots. Professional photographers often use the same equipment as amateurs, but their experience and quick reactions enable them to get much better images.

Camcorders

Lights! Camera! Action! Just a few years ago, it was only the directors of big-budget Hollywood movies who set the cameras rolling with these words. But today anyone can be a movie director. Digital camcorders that produce movies that are good enough to broadcast are small and cheap—and you can buy them in many stores. It is easy to edit movies too, with simple-to-use software that can help you cut out the boring shots, add a sound track, and then transfer your masterpiece onto a DVD.

eyepiece

removable battery unit

LCD (liquid-crystal display)

◀ Before video camcorders became popular and cheap, watching home movies meant closing the curtains, setting up a screen, and threading loops of film through a projector.

Film

Home movies did not begin with video, but with film. Eager amateurs used small cameras to film their families as early as 1900. Home movies became very popular in the 1960s with the introduction of Super-8 cameras. They were simple to use, and the film they shot came sealed inside an easy-load cartridge. However, like earlier home movies, Super-8 films were expensive and hard to edit. You could not see what you had shot until you processed the film and projected it.

The arrival of video

Video changed all of this—it let you see your movie immediately on a TV set, and you could reuse the tape. The first home video cameras had thick cables in order to tie together the cameras and recorders. All-in-one camcorders were the idea of Jerome Lemelson (1923–1997). The first, the Sony Betamovie, appeared in 1982. It was as big as a phone book!

microphone

digital videotape

image sensor

lens

▲ Editing a movie at home is now as simple as dragging and dropping icons on a computer screen. Besides changing the order of the shots, you can add special effects such as fading from one shot to another and creating animated titles. Mixing in music is simple too. And once the movie is finished, you can transfer it onto a DVD to show to friends and family.

▲ Although camcorders come in many shapes and sizes, most share the same basic features. A zoom lens at the front focuses a picture on the image sensor. This turns the light into an electronic signal that the camera can process and store on a digital videotape or disk. The eyepiece and LCD show you what you are filming, and a rechargeable battery powers everything.

◄ Video cameras are simple enough for children to use— but adults may need some help!

Digital camcorders

Digital technology made today's compact camcorders possible. By storing images as computer data, they squeeze an hour-long video onto a tiny cassette. Because the images are digital, you can store and edit them on your computer, just like any other digital file. Aspiring directors have been quick to see the advantages of tiny, cheap camcorders. They have used them to make low-budget movies. Some have had startling success—*The Blair Witch Project* (1999), made for only $40,000, earned its makers more than $100 million.

▲ The 1978 arcade game *Space Invaders* had crude graphics, but few people could resist shooting down advancing aliens! It was so popular that some Japanese cities ran out of the 100-yen coins that players fed into the machines.

▼ The first home consoles came with a selection of software. Most of it was dull and slow compared to today's games. This boy is playing tic-tac-toe in the mid-1970s.

Computer games

Jumping and running through grungy cityscapes or battlings evil foes, characters in modern computer games are so slick and realistic that they look almost alive. No longer child's play, games are difficult to master and have plots that keep even adults glued to the screen. The games depend on modern computer power for their spectacular effects. Not long ago, when computers were slower and simpler, on-screen characters were simple stick figures, and the only sports simulations were crude ping-pong games.

The first computer game

Almost as soon as computers had screens, programmers began writing computer games. The first game was the 1962 creation of Stephen Russell (born 1937), a student at the Massachusetts Institute of Technology (MIT). In the game, two simple spacecraft (triangles) fired torpedoes (dots) at each other as they orbited a planet (circle). Called *Spacewar*, the game was addictive, but it needed a computer that cost the equivalent of six years' salary for a programmer.

Arcade machines

Arcade (coin-operated) games began with ping-pong. Even simpler than *Spacewar*, *Pong* used lines for bats and a square for a ball, but it became hugely popular. The invention of American Nolan Bushnell (born 1943), *Pong* launched the computer-game industry. Home computer-game consoles that plugged into TV sets first appeared in 1972.

▼ Sony's handheld PSP (PlayStation Portable) has better graphics than most business computers.

▲ It takes many different skills to create a good computer game. While electronic aids help programmers create convincing characters, there is still no substitute for an artist's drawing ability.

High-tech consoles

Today the fastest and most exciting computer games run on consoles. Designed for realism and speed, they have the most advanced image-processing chips in order to create smooth, quickly changing graphics. Linked to other players by cordless controllers or over the Internet, players can compete with their best friends—or with strangers they may never meet!

▶ Computer games are not just for children. Adults play them; the game industry makes more money than the movie business, and game heroes often end up in movies. Gun-waving characters, such as Lara Croft (right), worry parents, but simulation games, such as *The Sims,* have shown that fast cars, blood, and gore are not essential for success.

Music

What type of music is on the sound track to your life? Rock? Rap? R & B? Jazz? If you have a personal music player such as an iPod, you can listen to whatever you want, wherever you are. And you can pick and choose tracks from online libraries that offer an almost limitless range of tunes. But access to music was not always this easy, and music players were not always small and personal.

◄ In 1877 Thomas Edison invented the phonograph, the first machine that both played and recorded music. A needle moved over a rotating, grooved cylinder, producing music from a large wooden horn.

Cylinders and records

For most of the 1900s, the gramophone, invented by Emile Berliner (1851–1925) in 1888, dominated music in the home. This machine was similar to Thomas Edison's phonograph (see above, right) but played records rather than cylinders. Today DJs (disc jockeys) still spin vinyl records on turntables, but most people want a smaller, less fragile way to store music.

▲ Sony's Walkman was introduced in 1979. It was the first truly pocket-size personal music player, and it had amazing sound quality. It changed the way that people listened to music and *where* they could listen to it. Its headphones also meant that only *you* heard the music that you had chosen.

Portable music

Transistor radios launched portable music in the 1950s, but you could not choose what you listened to. It was not until 1963—and the invention of the cassette tape—that music players became truly personal. Even then, they were hardly portable; a clunky tape player was the size of a large book, and there was only one speaker that produced a tinny sound.

Cassette tapes were convenient, but they were technically a step backward. To cram an hour of music onto each one, the tape had to move slowly through the player, creating a horrible hiss that clever electronics fought hard to reduce.

Digital music

The invention of compact discs (CDs) in 1983 introduced high-quality music that was truly reliable for the first time. CDs stored music as digital data—a series of ones and zeroes—encoded as microscopic "pits" on the disc's shiny surface and then read by a laser beam. CDs sound no better than records played on the best hi-fi systems, but CDs were better at resisting scratches and dust. Within ten years, CD sales overtook sales of records and cassettes. Soon only DJs and hi-fi buffs were spinning the large black records.

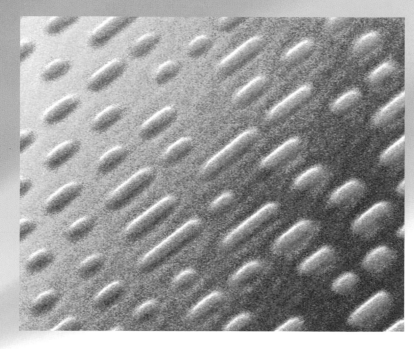

▲ Pressed onto the surface of a shiny CD, tiny pits record the music. A laser beam shines a spot of light onto the CD's surface, and when the CD spins, the pits—and the reflective areas in between them—create a flashing code that the CD player reads as digital data. A computer within the player converts the code back into sound.

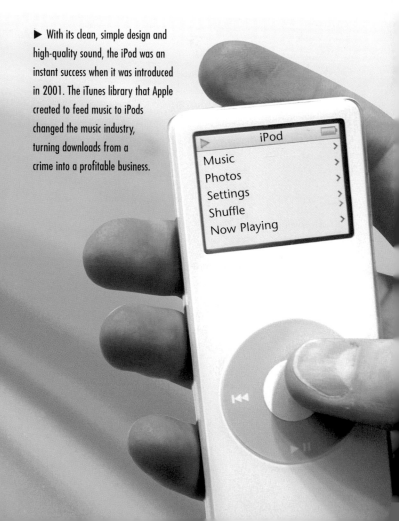

► With its clean, simple design and high-quality sound, the iPod was an instant success when it was introduced in 2001. The iTunes library that Apple created to feed music to iPods changed the music industry, turning downloads from a crime into a profitable business.

Downloading and sharing

CDs did not really change how people bought and listened to music. It took the Internet to do that. Music fans were fed up with overpriced albums padded with second-rate tracks. So they began sharing files—illegally—on the Internet. A new file format helped. Encoding tracks as MP3s cut their size by nine tenths. MP3 players, introduced in 1998, moved music away from computers and into listeners' pockets. Shaken by the popularity of "file sharing," the music industry finally began selling music online in 2003. Today the Internet is the largest music store in the world, selling millions of tracks and albums.

SUMMARY OF CHAPTER 2: TECHNOLOGY IN THE HOME

Powering up our lives

We depend on electric power. It lights our homes and often heats them too. It powers appliances that make our lives more comfortable. Scientists working around 130 years ago devised the basic inventions that brought electricity into the home. They not only created household appliances such as lightbulbs, but they also had to find ways of making and distributing electricity. While we now cannot manage without electricity, our need for power is causing problems. We must all use less to prevent our planet from overheating.

Recording our memories

The newest modern cameras are like fast, clever computers, storing images and

A racing game on a Sony PSP (PlayStation Portable)

movies as digital files. The first "still" cameras were invented in France in 1839. They captured images of still objects on polished metal plates. Cameras quickly improved so that they could record moving subjects. Home video cameras are a recent invention, first appearing in the mid-1970s. Camcorders, a combination of video cameras and recorders, replaced the Super-8 film cameras, which were until then the favorite way to shoot home movies.

Music and entertainment

Computer games are almost as old as electronic computers. The first ran on colossal and expensive machines found only in laboratories. As computers got smaller and cheaper, arcade games appeared, running on coin-operated consoles. Home computer games followed in the 1970s. Today's games are pocket-size, but music players are even smaller—some MP3 players are no bigger than a pack of gum. These replaced portable CD players. And the CD players were an advance on cassette-tape players, which—together with transistor radios—started the portable music revolution in the 1950s and 1960s.

Go further . . .

 Visit Electricity Online at: http://library.thinkquest.org/28032

Create a color photograph from two black-and-white pictures: www.pbs.org/wgbh/amex/eastman/sfeature/color.html

Check out The American Museum of Photography: www.photography-museum.com

Play the world's first computer game, *Spacewar*, recreated at: http://lcs.www.media.mit.edu/groups/el/projects/spacewar/

Eyewitness: Music by Neil Ardley (Dorling Kindersley, 2002)

 Photographer's assistant Helps professional photographers in a studio and on location. Work includes setting up equipment and operating lights.

Digital-music Web developer Helps build interactive Web sites for digital music stores.

Electrical-power engineer Designs and organizes major electric-power projects, planning power generation and distribution systems.

Game developer Works as part of a team to develop the story, sound, and visual effects for new electronic games and writes program code for parts of the games.

Visit a museum where everything is electric, right down to the boot warmers! The Museum of Electricity The Old Power Station, Bargates Christchurch, Dorset BH23 1QE, U.K. Phone: +44 (0) 1202 480 467 www.scottish-southern.co.uk/museum

Trace the history and advances of photography at: Museum of Photographic Arts 1649 El Prado San Diego, CA 92101 Phone: (619) 238-7559 www.mopa.org

CHAPTER 3

Transportation

From the frozen wastelands of Antarctica to the searing deserts of North Africa, there is hardly anywhere on Earth's surface that people have not explored. Once remote and hard to get to, these places are now within reach of anyone who can afford the ticket—thanks to a bewildering variety of powerful vehicles. Some, such as fast motorboats, are simply improvements on traditional ways of traveling. However, the most exciting of today's super vehicles are the completely new inventions. Private spacecraft, for example, could soon be opening up space to wealthy tourists. Transportation in all of its forms gives us fantastic freedom and enjoyment, but there is a price to pay. Motor vehicles and aircraft choke our atmosphere with their fumes, causing climate change. Unless we invent vehicles that rely less on fossil fuels for power and thus produce less pollution, transportation will destroy the places that we most want to visit.

Cars

▲ Henry Ford and his son, Edsel, take a ride in one of his many versions of the Model T motorcar in around 1912.

We love them. We hate them. But we cannot give them up. Cars are essential to us. They give us the freedom to go anywhere and to live in remote places. But cars are a huge problem too. Their exhaust fumes pollute the atmosphere and may make our world too warm to live in. Today car manufacturers are trying to build vehicles that are kinder to the environment.

Cheaper cars

Only the very rich could afford the first cars, so in 1900 there were only 11,000 in the whole world (today there are around 500 million). Factory production of "motorcars" made them cheap enough for most people, and American motor pioneer Henry Ford (1863–1947) was among the first to build cars in large numbers. His factories began making the Model T Ford in 1908. Over the next 20 years, Ford made 15 million of them.

Robot cars

Today's cars don't have much in common with the Model T except for their wheels, engines, and drivers—and even the drivers may soon be unnecessary. Computer scientists are working to make cars that drive themselves. So far, these vehicles are only safe on empty desert roads. But if they could speed through traffic, they could make highways safer and travel more pleasant.

▲ In 2005, racing to win a $2 million prize, 23 robot cars drove themselves 131 mi. (212km) through the desert in Nevada. The winning car, "Stanley" (above, left), finished in less than seven hours. Laser range finders, video cameras, and six computers kept Stanley on course.

◄ Electric cars that drivers charge up at stations are no solution for climate change. Though the cars themselves do not cause pollution, power plants must burn fossil fuels in order to generate the electricity that tops up their batteries. "Hybrid" cars, such as the Toyota Prius, are better—they combine gasoline and electric motors to reduce fuel use. However, the only long-term solution is less driving and more public transportation.

"Greener" cars

When cars first appeared, people thought that they would cure pollution, not cause it. Before German engineer Gottlieb Daimler (1834–1900) invented gasoline-driven engines in 1884, transportation was powered by horses. And horse droppings were smelly and hard to clear from the streets! Today car manufacturers are aware of the harmful gases that gasoline engines produce and are looking for alternative power sources such as hydrogen, electricity, and solar energy.

▼ Scientists use crash-test dummies to study the forces exerted on people during car accidents.

Controlling traffic

As cars multiplied, inventors looked for ways to keep traffic moving safely. Electric traffic lights began operating in 1914 in the American city of Cleveland, Ohio. They had only two colors—red and green—and a buzzer, which sounded to warn when the lights were about to change. Reflective raised road studs, to separate lanes of traffic, were the 1933 invention of English road repairer Percy Shaw. The eyes of a cat shining in his headlights inspired the invention.

Trains

▲ George Stephenson's *Rocket* famously won an 1829 locomotive competition for a railroad linking Liverpool and Manchester in England.

Floating above its track as if it weighed nothing, the world's most advanced train can race along at four times the speed of a car. Few modern trains can match the Chinese magnetic levitation (maglev) system for speed and efficiency, but even ordinary trains share many of its advantages. Compared to cars, railroads are safer and less polluting—and they do not suffer from traffic jams. No wonder trains remain a popular form of transportation 200 years after they were invented.

The first trains

Miners in Germany pushed carts that ran on rails as early as 1519. And, by 1712, the first steam engines were also used in mines to pump out water. In 1803 British engineer Richard Trevithick (1771–1833) was the first person to combine steam power and rails in order to make a steam-powered locomotive. George Stephenson (1781–1848) later improved Trevithick's invention, and, by 1850, railroad lines linked many large towns in the U.K. and in other countries.

New locomotives

Steam powered most trains until 1913, when diesel locomotives began to pull trucks and carriages. The new diesel engines burned oil to power pistons directly—rather than to make steam, which in turn pushed the pistons. This meant that a diesel locomotive used one half as much fuel as a steam locomotive pulling a similar train. Diesel engines still power many of the world's trains, except on the busiest lines.

▲ Freight trains (trains that transport goods), such as this one in Jordan, can move enormous loads over very long distances. Rail transportation, compared to road transportation, is safer, cheaper, and less harmful to the environment—a typical freight train can carry 50 truckloads over the same route.

Electric power

The most efficient way of powering trains is with electricity. However, supplying power through an extra rail or on an overhead wire makes electric railroad lines expensive to build. The first electric trains transported passengers in city areas and underground (where smoke from steam locomotives caused problems). Today electricity powers the most advanced rail networks, including the high-speed lines on which trains travel at almost 125 mph (200km/h).

Maglev trains

Electricity powers and lifts maglev trains. Electromagnets in the track push upward against magnets in the train, lifting it off the ground. More electromagnets push the carriages forward. Since the train does not touch anything, only friction with the air slows it down. Maglev trains do not need wheels at high speeds, but some of them do use wheels when traveling slowly—and in case the power fails. Existing maglev trains whiz along at up to 267 mph (430km/h)—future trains may go as fast as a jet aircraft.

▲ "Funicular" trains operate on steep slopes. They are hauled up on a cable that is pulled by an engine at the top of a hill. Instead of this cable, some mountain railroads have a third, toothed rail (between the two normal rails) that the cogwheels on the train grip onto.

▼ The Shanghai maglev train in China floats 0.4 in. (1cm) above its tracks.

Sea vehicles

Like a watery highway, the oceans link the continents with a vast, free transportation route. Immense cargo ships slowly carry goods around the world, while hovercrafts and hydrofoils ferry passengers and vehicles at much faster speeds, skimming above the waves. Though we have been sailing across the ocean's surface for more than 6,000 years, we began journeys beneath it less than 200 years ago. Today submarines can withstand the crushing pressure, cold, and constant darkness to reach the deepest ocean floor.

▲ This old sketch shows one of the first-ever submarines. It was built by Dutch inventor Cornelius Drebbel (1572–1633) in the 1620s. Powered by oars, the sub traveled up London's Thames river, in England, around 13 ft. (4m) underwater. The crew breathed air through tubes that reached up to the surface.

▶ The smallest submarines, or submersibles, do not even need crews; controlled from afar, they can go deeper without risking lives.

How submarines work

Before deep-sea submarines were possible, inventors had to solve the problems of pressure, power, air supply, and waterproofing. Early subs had weak hulls made out of greased leather, so they could not dive deep. However, modern submarines are strong enough to resist the crushing weight of the water above. Instead of oars, they are powered by motors that do not need air in order to work. Subs carry their own air supply, and to surface or dive, the crews fill "ballast tanks" with either air or seawater to change the submarines' weight.

War under the waves

Most submarines are used for warfare. Under the waves, submarines are invisible and can creep up undetected on enemy ships. Ordinary submarines have to surface regularly to stock up on air for the crew to breathe and to recharge their batteries. Nuclear submarines do not have these problems. Their power plants don't need air in order to work, and air for breathing is recycled. A nuclear sub could sail around the world seven times before its power ran out.

◀ On the surface, a mother ship steers a tiny, uncrewed submersible. A flexible tether links the two vessels. The tether combines data and power cables. The data cable enables scientists on the mother ship to control the sub's thrusters, which push it forward. It also allows them to watch pictures from onboard video cameras.

On the surface

Hovercrafts, invented in 1952 by Christopher Cockerell (1910–1999), float on a cushion of air. They work as well on mud, ice, and quicksand as they do on the sea. Hydrofoils reduce the friction that slows them down by rising out of the water. An undersea "wing" raises the hull, just as a regular wing lifts a plane into the air.

▲ Modern ocean liners, such as the *Queen Mary 2,* are like luxurious floating cities. With space for more than 2,600 passengers, the ship has a movie theater and a virtual golf course. Its power plant could provide enough electricity to light 200,000 homes.

▼ A hovercraft's ability to move freely on almost any surface makes it a useful vehicle where land meets water. This hovercraft is used for ocean rescue off the U.K.'s northwest coast. It can cross shallow water and mud that would stop an ordinary lifeboat.

Aviation

At a windy airport, a huge aircraft powers down the runway and, with a deafening roar, is blasted into the air by its four huge engines. The Airbus A380 is a "superjumbo" and the world's largest passenger airliner, even larger than the Boeing 747, which ruled the skies for 35 years. Powerful jet aircraft make travel so safe, quick, and easy that we forget just how amazing it is to fly. Yet it is hardly more than 100 years since the Wright brothers, Orville and Wilbur, invented aviation.

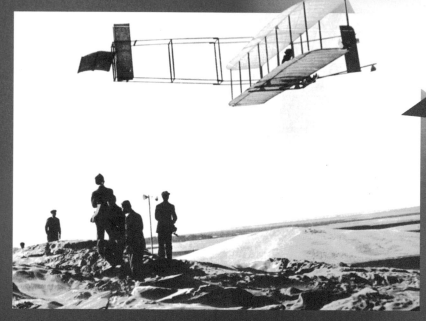

▲ Two American bicycle engineers from Dayton, Ohio, were the first to build a working aircraft. One week before Christmas in 1903, Orville (1871–1948) and Wilbur (1867–1912) Wright powered up the engine on *Flyer*, and Orville took off from the sand at Kill Devil Hill on North Carolina's windy coast. Their longest flight that day lasted only 59 seconds, but it earned them a place in history. This picture shows an improved Wright aircraft flying over Kill Devil Hill in 1911.

Giants of the air

It is not easy to grasp the sheer scale of an airliner. At almost 240 ft. (73m), the A380 is longer than eight buses. It can move the population of a small town 9,000 mi. (15,000km) without landing to refuel. But the A380 is a toy compared to the biggest of the world's aircraft. The airships that ferried passengers across the Atlantic Ocean in the 1930s were three times as long. Their passenger cabins hung beneath gigantic balloons, held in place by aluminum frames.

▲ Airships seemed like the future of aviation in the 1930s—until the huge *Hindenburg* burst into flames in Lakehurst, New Jersey, in 1937. After the accident, few travelers dared to fly in a balloon.

▲ Built to show off the engineering skills of the U.K. and France, *Concorde* flew the wealthy across the Atlantic Ocean for 27 years. Because of the air and noise pollution that supersonic airliners cause, there will probably never be another aircraft like it.

◀ The newest warplanes are invisible weapons. Stealth technology hides them from radar— the radio detection system used to aim antiaircraft defenses. To reduce its radar reflection, this Lockheed F-117A Nighthawk has sharp angles and is covered in radar-absorbing paint. Unfortunately, the paint runs off in the rain, so the F-117A only operates on sunny days!

Faster and higher

No aircraft is ever fast enough for impatient passengers. So, in the 1950s, aviation companies began designing planes to fly faster than the speed of sound. *Concorde*, built jointly by the U.K. and France, first flew passengers in 1976. Traveling at 1,345 mph (2,170km/h) (around twice the speed of sound), it only took 3.5 hours to cross the Atlantic Ocean from Paris, France, or London, England, to New York City. Unfortunately, at full speed the aircraft was too noisy to fly over areas where people lived, which is one of the reasons why it never made any money.

▼ The round radar dome above the rotor of this AH-64 Apache helicopter allows the pilot to "look over" a building or hilltop and fire deadly weapons while hovering out of sight.

Flying windmills

An ordinary aircraft needs a long runway in order to pick up speed because it relies on air rushing quickly over its wings to lift it. However, a helicopter spins its wings to get the rush of air that it needs to fly— so it can take off from small spaces. Italian artist and inventor Leonardo da Vinci sketched a helicopter in the 1400s, but it took until the 1900s for the first "chopper" to fly—built by French bicycle engineer Paul Cornu in 1907. Modern helicopters do a variety of jobs that would be impossible for fixed-wing aircraft. They can land on oil rigs, ships, and hospital roofs; they can carry rock stars to gigs; and they can transport troops and equipment in and out of remote war zones.

Space travel

Traveling into space and floating weightlessly, high up above Earth, once seemed like a ridiculous dream, but for astronauts on the space shuttle, it has become almost routine. Though just seven lucky astronauts fly in each shuttle, space travel may soon become the newest white-knuckle ride. If private space vehicles like *SpaceShipOne* succeed, space tourism will be within reach of anyone who can afford a ticket.

▲ The first space passenger vehicle was the Russian *Vostok 1* capsule launched in 1961. Cosmonaut (Russian pilot) Yuri Gagarin (1934–1968) was really just cargo—he had no control over the course that his capsule took. *Vostok 1* circled Earth once while Gagarin looked out of a porthole—". . . Earth is bluish," he commented.

▼ The space shuttle *Discovery* is prepared for launch at the Kennedy Space Center, in Florida, in June 2005. The shuttle rides piggyback on two solid fuel rocket boosters and a giant tank (orange in this picture) that fuels the shuttle's own rocket engines.

The X PRIZE

The $10-million X PRIZE was set up to encourage private space flights. To win it, a space vehicle had to fly into space (60 mi./100km above Earth) with a crew of three people, return safely, and then repeat the journey within two weeks. A small U.S. company won the prize in October 2004 with *SpaceShipOne*. A lightweight jet aircraft, *White Knight*, carried the craft up 9.4 mi. (15.2km) before *SpaceShipOne*'s rocket engine fired and blasted it to the edge of outer space.

◀ *SpaceShipOne* hangs beneath its jet aircraft mother ship, *White Knight*. The two aircraft have identical cockpits, but *SpaceShipOne* has a rocket motor that powers it into space.

Reusable spacecraft

Less than one month after Yuri Gagarin became the first person in space, NASA (the U.S.'s National Aeronautics and Space Administration) launched its own space vehicle, *Freedom 7*. Its pilot, Alan Shepard (1923–1998), experienced weightlessness for five minutes before his capsule splashed safely into the Atlantic Ocean.

In 1981, 20 years after Gagarin's space flight, NASA launched the first space shuttle, *Columbia*. The shuttle was designed to be reused. When friction with the air heats an ordinary spacecraft on its return to Earth, its outer layer burns up. The shuttle, however, resisted the heat with a covering of ceramic tiles. The shuttle was successful, but there have been deadly accidents—in 2003, for example, *Columbia* exploded on its return to Earth.

Sailing through space

Future space probes may not need rocket fuel; instead they could be blown along with a sail. Space is a vacuum—there is no air and, therefore, no wind. However, light from the Sun creates a tiny bit of pressure on everything that it touches. By unfolding a giant sail, a spacecraft could use this "radiation pressure" to power it across huge distances. Scientists predict that the craft's speed could reach 37 mi. (60km) per second, but they have yet to test their ideas. The first space sailing ship crashed during its launch in 2005.

▶ The pressure from sunlight that pushes a solar sail along is tiny—the equivalent to 0.53 oz. (15g) in weight pushing on an area the size of a soccer field. So the sail has to be huge, as this example from NASA shows. Even with a giant sail, spacecraft powered by radiation pressure would gather speed very slowly.

SUMMARY OF CHAPTER 3: TRANSPORTATION

On roads and rails

The invention of gas-powered engines in the late 1800s made cars possible, and, within only 40 years, they had almost replaced horse transportation. Though cars give travelers a lot of freedom, their exhaust fumes damage our planet's climate. Today carmakers are looking for alternative fuels, such as electricity, to limit the damage. Rail transportation is kinder to the environment and frees travelers from the stress of traffic jams. Invented almost 100 years before cars, railroad locomotives were at first powered by steam. Diesel and electric motors replaced steam in the 1900s. Today trains are the quickest form of land transportation. The most modern don't need wheels and are almost as fast as aircraft.

An electric car recharges its batteries

Ships, submarines, and hydrofoils

Sea transportation is slow but efficient; ships carry huge cargoes at low cost. Their basic shape has hardly changed since the first craft sailed the oceans 6,000 years ago, but today the source of a ship's power is an oil-fired engine, not a sail. Special types of ships have made sea transportation more versatile. Submarines lurk below the waves to make war or explore ocean depths, and hydrofoils skim just above the surface.

Air and space travel

Soaring high up in the atmosphere—and above it—planes and spacecraft are the fastest way of getting around. They are the newest type of transportation too—nobody flew until 1903. Today flight is routine, with huge aircraft moving vacationers around the world at low cost. Space travel only began in 1961 and is still a dangerous adventure. New space planes aim to give wealthy tourists a taste of travel beyond the atmosphere. Journeys to other planets—perhaps with beams of light for power—remain a distant dream.

Go further . . .

Find out how we will get around in the years to come at Future Transport: http://library.thinkquest.org/04oct/01249

Discover fuel cells powered by hydrogen gas—could they be the power source for cars of the future? www.pbs.org/wgbh/nova/sciencenow/3210/01.html

Enjoy a colorful look at the history of air transportation: www.century-of-flight.freeola.com

Eyewitness: Boat by Eric Kentley (Dorling Kindersley, 2000)

The World of Flight by Ian Graham (Kingfisher, 2006)

Automotive engineer
Member of a large team that designs, develops, and tests new vehicles.

Train driver
Operates trains, checks fuel on nonelectric locomotives, and performs minor maintenance tasks.

Naval architect
Designs new ships and oceangoing equipment and organizes their manufacture.

Space-vehicle engineer
Develops ideas for new space vehicles and cooperates with other engineers to design and build the most practical craft.

Visit an aerospace museum: Smithsonian National Air and Space Museum Independence Avenue at 4th Street, SW Washington, D.C. 20560 Phone: (202) 633-1000 www.nasm.si.edu

Learn about the birthplace of American railroading at: Baltimore & Ohio Railroad Museum 910 West Pratt Street Baltimore, MD 21223 Phone: (410) 752-2490 www.borail.org

Visit a collection of early streetcars at the Seashore Trolley Museum in Kennebunkport, ME www.trolleymuseum.org

CHAPTER 4

New technology

Inventions affect our lives in many unexpected and unseen ways, both big and small. Behind the doors of enormous factories, for example, technology has transformed the way that things are made, with robots building everything from cars to TV sets. Inventors have been at work on a minute scale as well. In medicine, researchers operate at the level of a single cell to create clones (identical copies of plants and animals). They snip and join tiny strands of DNA—the ropelike molecule that controls everything about us.

Pharmaceutical researchers have made us healthier, with medicines and vaccines to prolong our lives. Another new branch of technology deals with ever-smaller devices. Scarcely bigger than dust, nanomachines are too small to be seen without a microscope. In the future, they could perform all types of amazing services—and even build themselves, atom by atom.

**Colored X-ray image
of a microscope**

Robotics

Imagine a worker who can do a complicated job 24 hours each day, without sleep, food, or breaks. Or who can withstand deadly radiation to make repairs inside a damaged nuclear power plant. These workers do not exist, but a robot could easily do these jobs. Most robots work in factories, assembling cars and electronic equipment. A few do dangerous jobs such as making bombs safe or exploring space. And domestic robots can clean our floors and mow our lawns.

▲ This automaton was built in around 1875 and was called *Psycho*. A form of after-dinner entertainment, it attempted to read the minds of its wealthy audience members. Most of these mechanical toys in the 1700s and 1800s mimicked humans or animals.

▼ Factory robots, like these automatic welders, have replaced human workers on many dull and dangerous tasks. The success of robots led experts to predict that future factories would not need lighting or heating because their workers would all be machines. However, this has not happened—robots are still not reliable enough to work on their own, and nobody has yet made a robot that can repair other robots!

From toy to worker

Robots began as mechanical toys in the 1700s, built to amuse wealthy people. Very simple systems for controlling machines were invented at around the same time. Robots were called "automata" or "androids" until 1920, when Czech author Karel Capek (1890–1938) wrote about mechanical workers in his play *R.U.R.* He named them after the Czech word *robota*, meaning "hard, boring work." Real robots that could be programmed to perform different tasks were not practical until computers were made available to control them in the 1960s.

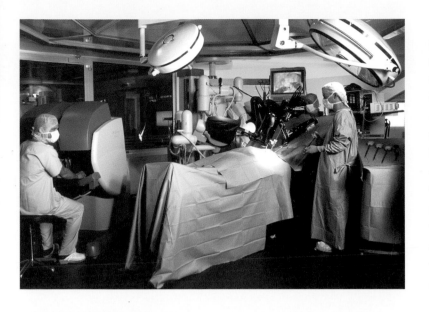

◄ To operate using the da Vinci surgery robot, a surgeon sitting at a console (on the left of this picture) looks into twin eyepieces like a pair of binoculars. These show a three-dimensional image produced by a pair of cameras positioned inside the patient's body. By moving the handles inside the console, the surgeon controls the instruments next to the cameras to grab, move, or cut tissue.

Automatic surgery

Letting a robot loose with a scalpel may not sound like a good idea, but growing numbers of robots work in operating rooms. Under the control of a surgeon on the other side of the room, robot arms grip and cut the patient's body. Tiny cameras give the surgeon a close-up view in three dimensions. Robot surgery has many advantages—robots' hands can reach through tiny holes, so scars are smaller, and they are completely steady, making cuts more precise.

Industrial robots

Putting together cars or computers is dull, hard work, and single-arm robots have replaced humans in many factories. Robots can lift, weld, and spray paint cars faster and better than people can. To program them, real workers first move the arms, "teaching" the robot what to do. The robot can then repeat exactly the same action millions of times. Cameras give robots vision so that they can identify the parts to be assembled.

▼ Honda's *Asimo* is one of the first android (humanlike) robots that can mimic human movements such as walking up stairs. Android robots are being developed by car manufacturers to help around the home or office. Currently, the most successful cleaning robot is probably the disk-shaped *Roomba*, which vacuums floors while its owners are out. "Social robots," disguised as dogs or dinosaurs, are intelligent toys that are strictly for entertainment.

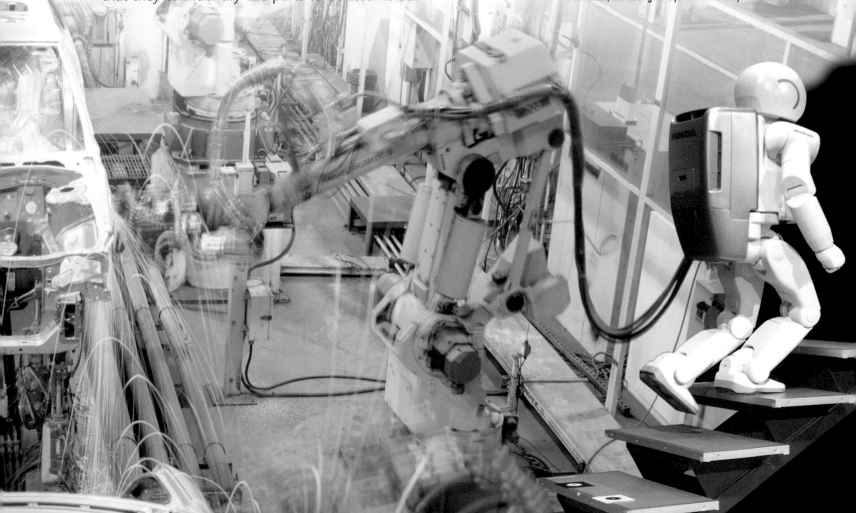

Nanotechnology

Think of the smallest speck of dust that you can see. Now picture something 100,000 times smaller. Particles this size are the building blocks for one of the newest, smallest ways of making things: nanotechnology. In the distant future, nanotechnology could create machines that assemble themselves from individual atoms—the smallest particles that make up everything in our world.

▲ Nanotechnology is already in action in some very useful—if undramatic—ways. By using much tinier particles in industry, highly durable and stain-resistant fabrics can be produced, as well as super filters that remove germs from water and clear sunscreen to protect against sunburn.

▼ Carbon nanotubes, shown here magnified around six million times, have peculiar properties. Injected into the cells of living things, they head straight for the nucleus—the vital center that controls growth and reproduction. Researchers believe that they will soon be able to use this ability to target medicine at the part of the cell where it will do the most good.

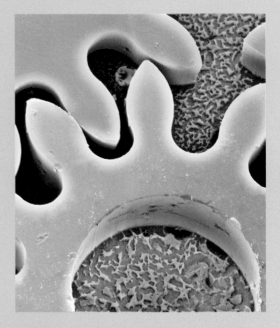

▲ Visible under a microscope, microcogs work together to form a microgear mechanism. These mechanisms are used in everything from ink-jet printer cartridges to disposable blood-pressure monitors.

Tiny gears

Strictly speaking, nanotechnology describes devices around one millionth of a millimeter in size. However, the word is often used to cover larger inventions such as MEMS (microelectromechanical systems). Though they are not strictly on a "nano" scale, you still need a powerful magnifier to see them clearly. MEMS are made just like computer chips by depositing or etching patterns onto a wafer of silicon. There is a MEMS device in every new car. It triggers the air bags in an accident. Just as important, it ensures that the air bags do not open when the driver simply brakes hard.

Carbon nanotubes

What do a pencil mark and a diamond have in common? Quite a lot—both are forms of carbon. Carbon can also exist in a third, recently discovered form, as narrow tubes (nanotubes) or tiny balls (buckyballs). Nanotubes are 50,000 times narrower than a human hair, but may be several inches long. Their shape and structure give them immense strength and unusual electrical properties. A rope made out of carbon nanotubes could hoist satellites into space, and they are already being used to make electric motors more reliable. One day, they may help pharmacists deliver medicine only to diseased cells.

◄ In this imaginative computer image, nanorobots swarm on a brain cell, preparing to inject it with a healing drug. Before such ideas can become reality, scientists must find ways to make and control these tiny devices.

The molecular factory

Scientists already use atomic-force microscopes to arrange atoms one by one. With this technique, they could possibly build "nanomachines" that are small enough to operate inside a living cell—but it would take a very long time. To speed up the process, they aim to create a device that can copy itself over and over again. Nanotechnology fans predict that the tiny devices will perform surgery from inside our bodies, swimming in arteries to control heart-stopping blood clots. At the moment, such ideas are pure science fiction, not reality.

Genetic engineering

Inside your body's cells is a biological code describing you—and only you—in the tiniest details. Called deoxyribonucleic acid—"DNA" for short—it is shaped like a 6.5-ft. (2-m)-long coiled rope. All living things rely on DNA to pass on information, in the form of genes, from parent to child. By decoding DNA for plants, humans, and other animals, scientists have invented a powerful tool. With genetic engineering, we might make crops grow on wasteland or cure the world's most feared diseases.

Cracking the code

The coiled-rope shape of DNA was the 1953 discovery of James Watson (born 1928) and Francis Crick (1916–2004). Soon after their breakthrough, scientists began to sequence (decode) DNA to find its structure. Understanding the "genetic code" of living things enables us to change them. For example, by moving genes from Arctic fish to tomatoes, scientists hoped to create a frost-resistant crop. They failed, but other, similar "genetic modifications" (GMs) have worked, making plants that resist diseases or that taste better.

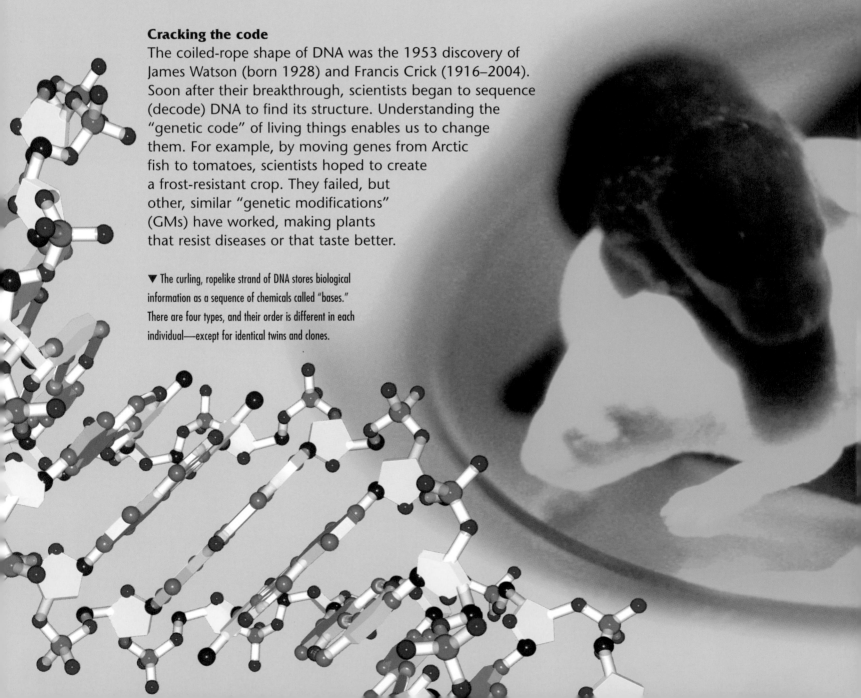

▼ The curling, ropelike strand of DNA stores biological information as a sequence of chemicals called "bases." There are four types, and their order is different in each individual—except for identical twins and clones.

▼ By moving genes from glowing jellyfish into mice, scientists have bred mice that glow when they are lit up by a beam of ultraviolet light, which is not normally visible to the naked eye. These transgenic mice are not novelty pets—the research has a serious purpose. By making cancer cells glow in the same way, doctors could trace—and stop—their deadly progress throughout the body.

Making identical twins

By taking the part of a cell containing DNA—the nucleus—and implanting it into a developing cell that lacks a nucleus, scientists can create copies of plants and animals. This method, called cloning, produced identical frogs in the 1950s. Successful cloning of mammals began in 1984. Scientists hope to make identical twins of the best farm animals in order to provide more and better milk, meat, or wool.

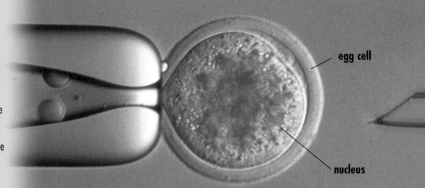

▶ In the first stage of the cloning process, researchers remove the DNA from a sheep egg cell (center). Suction holds the cell firmly against the tube on the left. The sharp glass tube on the right will puncture the cell's outer wall and suck out the nucleus that contains the DNA.

egg cell

nucleus

◀ In 1996 scientists at Scotland's Roslin Institute were the first people to produce clones from cells taken from an adult mammal. The result was Dolly the sheep, shown here on the right. Clones such as Dolly could one day be used as living "drug factories," producing disease-fighting proteins in their milk.

◀ Big chemical companies want farmers to grow genetically modified crops, such as this GM rapeseed, because it can resist the weed killer that the companies also sell. However, the extended use of a weed killer can cause plants to become resistant to it. If this resistance spreads to a weed called charlock, rapeseed's wild relative, the charlock would spread quickly and be very difficult to control.

Should we do it?

Not everyone agrees that tinkering with DNA is a good idea. Resistant to weed killers, genetically modified (GM) crops, for example, have encouraged farmers to spray their fields more often, killing wildlife. Crops may also cross (breed with) weeds, creating "superweeds" that no spray can kill. Critics oppose cloning because they believe that it will lead to cloned humans. They fear that by combining genetic modification with cloning, scientists might create "designer babies," with only the qualities that parents want.

Medical technology

An American baby born in 1900 could expect to die 47 years later; a child born today will live—on average—to be 77. Why do we live so much longer now? Improvements in medicine are the most important reason. In only 100 years, researchers have found vaccines to protect us against many deadly diseases, and they have discovered new types of medicines to prevent infections. New medical technology enables us to restart a failing heart or to spot cancer deep inside the brain.

▶ Traditional Chinese herbal remedies can help heal diseases that "modern" medicine cannot. The Chinese cures contain dozens of chemicals, some that work only when combined. Researchers hope to identify which are the healing chemicals so that they can make cures more effective and reduce harmful side effects.

Molds and medicines

The pharmaceutical (medicinal drugs) industry today uses genetic engineering (see pages 54–55) to tailor treatments to each patient. This lifesaving business relies on constant research by observant scientists. In 1928 one scientist, Alexander Fleming (1881–1955), discovered penicillin, the first antibiotic. Since then, antibiotics have saved millions of lives by stopping infections.

▶ Penicillin grows in a laboratory dish

▲ When Alexander Fleming was working in his laboratory in 1928, he noticed that some mold on one of his dishes was killing the germs around it. When purified, this mold became penicillin.

Medical imaging

The discovery of X-rays in 1895, by German physicist Wilhelm Röntgen (1845–1923), greatly aided the medical profession. X-rays gave a good view of the hard parts of the body, especially bones, but the invention of computers made them much more useful. Computerized axial tomography (CAT) scanners, invented in 1972, formed X-ray images of narrow sections of the body, creating a 3-D picture that showed the soft tissues clearly.

▶ Positron-emission tomography (PET), developed in 1974, and magnetic resonance imaging (MRI) scanners, developed in 1977, further improved internal images of the human body. Here (right) an MRI scanner produces cross-sectional images of a patient's brain.

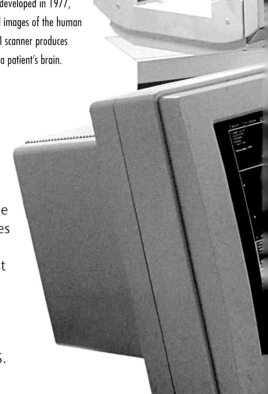

Shots for protection

One shot can give years of immunity (protection) against a disease. This technique of vaccination, discovered in the 1700s, relies on infecting patients with a vaccine—a weakened form of a disease. The world's first vaccination gave immunity from smallpox. Today there are vaccines against diseases such as measles and polio, but the search is still on for a vaccine against HIV (human immunodeficiency virus), which causes AIDS.

Caring for the developing world

Medicines began as herbal cures. Even today, one fourth of all drugs comes from plants. People in wealthy countries benefit from both chemical and plant-based medicines, while many people who live in poorer parts of the world only have access to traditional medicines. Each year, $4,000 is spent on one American person's health care, but only $20 is spent on an African's. Fortunately, a few charities are trying to change this. Business tycoon Bill Gates (born 1955), the chairman of the world-famous Microsoft Corporation, is investing money in the search for a cure for malaria, a deadly disease that mostly affects poor countries.

▲ A woman in Malaysian Borneo picks a plant that local people use to relieve pain and to treat skin diseases. People who live in rain-forest regions all over the world use plants to treat their illnesses. Drug researchers try to tap into this knowledge so that the wider world can benefit.

SUMMARY OF CHAPTER 4: NEW TECHNOLOGY

Obedient machines

Robots began in the 1700s as amusing toys. Today robots that perform useful jobs surround us. In the home, they wash dishes or vacuum the floor. In industry, robots build and paint cars and assemble electronic parts. And in war

zones or nuclear power plants, robots work in conditions that are too dangerous for humans. Almost all robots do only one job, and they do it very well. Android robots that can do everything for us remain a laboratory dream.

An android robot sophisticated enough to walk up stairs

Small is beautiful

A tiny revolution is transforming industry. Nanotechnology is engineering on a microscopic scale. Scientists are already using it to create ultrafine coatings, powders, and filters, extra-strong materials, and miniature mechanical devices. Some people believe that in the distant future nanotechnology will allow us to build things atom by atom, assembling robots that are too small to see. They hope that these minute machines will even learn to assemble themselves.

Genetically better?

By decoding our DNA—the "blueprint" for all human life—scientists have found a new and powerful way of promoting health and conquering diseases. Genetic techniques are the latest of many medical breakthroughs that have helped us live longer. These include medical imaging such as X-rays and CAT scans, vaccinations, and powerful medicines made from molds and plants. The citizens of wealthy nations have benefited more from these advances than those in the developing world.

The growing knowledge of the genes of animals and plants has allowed researchers to create genetically modified, "designer" species. However, there is bitter opposition to this work and to the cloning of animals.

Go further . . .

Learn to guide a robot rover at: www.thetech.org/robotics

Visit a virtual exhibition about nanotechnology at London's Science Museum and play the NanoLand game: www.sciencemuseum.org.uk/antenna/nano

Become a DNA detective at this genetic site from the American Museum of Natural History: www.ology.amnh.org/genetics

Eyewitness: Robot by Roger Bridgman (Dorling Kindersley, 2004)

Genetic Engineering: The Facts by Sally Morgan (Evans Pub. Group, 2001)

Robotics engineer
Designs, builds, programs, and repairs robots for use in industry.

Plant geneticist
Breeds plants to produce varieties that give bigger or better crops or that grow in less-than-ideal conditions of soil or climate.

Medical-imaging technician
Develops software to process data from MRI scanners, producing clearer images that make diagnosis of diseases quicker and more accurate.

Nanowire synthesis researcher
Investigates nanowires—ultrathin wires that could help build the next generation of computers.

Learn about surgery in the past—no anesthesia! The Old Operating Theatre Museum, 9a St. Thomas's Street, London SE1 9RY, U.K. Phone: +44 (0) 20 7188 2679 www.thegarret.org.uk

Visit an exhibition about robots at: MIT Museum 265 Massachusetts Avenue Cambridge, MA 02139 Phone: (617) 253-4444 http://web.mit.edu/museum/index.html

Find out about Gregor Mendel, the pioneer of genetics, at: Mendel Museum, Augustinian Abbey Mendlovo námesti 1a CZ-603 00 Brno, Czech Republic www.mendel-museum.org

Glossary

animation
Making a movie from drawings or computer pictures that are different for each frame of the film, creating an illusion of movement.

antenna
Device that receives or transmits a radio signal.

antibiotic
Medical drug that stops infections caused by bacteria.

atmosphere
Mixture of gases that surrounds Earth, making life possible.

atom
The smallest particle of the material from which everything is made.

atomic-force microscope
Powerful microscope that forms images by measuring the attraction between the subject and a probe at its tip.

audio
Having to do with sound.

automatic
Happening without any action by people.

ballast tank
Tank that can be filled with air or water to change the weight of a craft.

CAD
Short for computer-aided design.

carbon
An element (basic substance) that exists in several forms: graphite, diamond, and nanotubes or buckyballs.

CD
Short for compact disc; a disc that stores information or music in the form of digital data.

circuit
Electrical device made up of parts such as transistors and connecting wires.

communication satellite
A satellite in orbit above Earth that passes on communication signals.

computer chip
A miniaturized circuit for processing data inside a computer.

console
A control panel for a computer, game device, or other machine.

DAB
Short for digital audio broadcasting.

An "antenna farm" in Arizona

data
Information, usually stored in a form that computers can understand.

diesel
Type of engine that makes fuel explode by "squeezing" it.

digital
Using data in the form of a string of on-off (one-zero) signals—rather than a continuous flow.

DNA
Short for deoxyribonucleic acid; the ropelike molecule that stores information about the shape and structure of living things.

DVD
Short for digital video disc; a disc that stores movies.

dynamo
A device that turns movement into electricity.

electric current
Form of energy that flows in a circuit to power useful devices or to operate a computer.

electronics
Use of electricity for communication or computing.

filament
Thin strand inside a lightbulb that glows when heated by electricity.

friction
The sticky force that stops objects from sliding when pressed together.

graphics
Pictures, especially those that make information visible.

hardware
The machinery of a computer—rather than software programs.

hi-fi
Short for high-fidelity (good quality) in recorded sound and music.

HTML
Short for hypertext markup language; the code used to write Web pages.

hydrogen
A very light gas that burns with explosive power.

image-processing chip
Part of a computer or game device that draws images on a screen.

integrated circuit
Miniature electronic part that contains many transistors and other devices on a silicon chip.

interface
The controls and display of a computer or game.

LCD
Short for liquid crystal display; the flat screen of a computer, a digital camera, and many other devices.

lens
Shaped piece of glass that gathers rays of light to form sharp pictures.

locomotive
The front part of a train, containing the engine, that pulls the carriages or trucks behind.

microprocessor
Chip that does most of the work in a computer.

A rusting locomotive no longer in service

microwave
Invisible form of energy, similar to light, used for cooking and communication.

molecule
Tiny group of similar or mixed atoms that cannot be separated without changing their qualities.

Morse code
Code of long and short pulses used to spell out the alphabet.

MP3
Method of storing music files and greatly reducing their size; also a name for the files themselves.

nano-
Prefix that divides by one billion the measurement unit that follows it.

nuclear
Based on the splitting of atoms to release great power.

online
Available from a computer network, especially the Internet.

optical fiber
Thin glass thread that carries data in the form of light.

pharmaceutical
Having to do with medicinal drugs.

piston
Metal block that slides back and forth in an engine, driven by steam or fuel.

quantum
To do with the fixed amounts of energy that atoms can possess.

radiation
Energy, such as light or microwaves, spreading as waves, particles, or rays.

radio
Form of invisible radiation commonly used for communication.

radio telescope
Telescope that studies the stars by looking at the radio waves they give off.

silicon
Chemical substance commonly found in sand that is purified and used to make computer chips.

software
The complex instructions that make a computer work.

stereo
Giving the illusion of depth in a picture or sound.

telegraphy
Way of communicating using pulses of electricity in Morse code.

transistor
Miniature electronic switch or amplifying part.

transistor radio
A miniature radio that works using transistors.

transmitter
Device that sends out a communication signal.

ultraviolet
Invisible radiation, given off by the Sun and by special lamps, that has more energy than visible light but less than X-rays.

A silicon chip

vaccine
Weakened form of a disease that, when absorbed by the body, provides protection against the disease itself.

vacuum
Space containing no air or any other substance.

valve
Device that allows a flow in only one direction.

VCR
Short for video cassette recorder.

video
Picture—especially a TV picture.

wavelength
Single channel of communication; or the gap between the highest levels in a wave.

Web
Short for World Wide Web; the simple system of pages and clickable links that makes the Internet easy to use.

Index

Acknowledgments

The publisher would like to thank the following for permission to reproduce their material. Every care has been taken to trace copyright holders. However, if there have been unintentional omissions or failure to trace copyright holders, we apologize and will, if informed, endeavor to make corrections in any future edition.

Key: b = bottom, c = center, l = left, r = right, t = top

Cover *front cover* Science Photo Library (SPL)/Roger Harris; pages 1 SPL/Sandia National Laboratories; 2–3 National Geographic Society (NGS)/David Lawrence/Panoramic Images; 4–5 NGS/H Takeuchi/Panoramic Images; 7 SPL/Gusto; 8–9 Photolibrary.com; 8*cl* Getty/Photographer's Choice; 9*tr* Corbis/George Shelley; 10–11 SPL/Gusto; 10*tr* SPL/Martin Dohrin; 11*br* SPL/Philippe Psaila; 12–13 Getty/Taxi; 12*tr* SPL; 12*b* Corbis/Bettmann; 13*br* Empics/AP; 14*l* Rex Features; 14*br* The Art Archive; 15*tl* Empics/AP; 15*b* SPL/Publiphoto; 16*tl* Empics/AP; 16*b* Corbis/zefa; 17*b* Alamy; 18*tr* Getty/Digital Vision; 18*bl* Photolibrary.com; 18–19 Alamy/Hugh Threlfall; 19*tr* Rex Features; 19*c* SPL/Leonard Lessin; 19*br* Getty/ AFP; 20–21 Getty/Iconica; 20*tl* Corbis/Bettmann; 20*bl* Getty/Hulton; 20*cr* SPL/Alexander Tsiaras; 21*tl* SPL/Mike Miller; 21*br* SPL/David Parker; 22–23 Kobal; 22*tl* SPL/Adam Hart-Davis; 23*tr* Rex Features; 23*c* Ronald Grant Archive; 23*b* Kobal; 24 SPL; 25 SPL/Hugh Turvey; 26*tl* SPL/Sheila Terry; 26–27 Getty/NGS; 27*t* Getty/Imagebank; 27*br* Getty/Taxi; 28*tl* Topfoto; 28*tr* DK Images; 28–29 Corbis/Schlegelmilch; 28*tl* Getty/Iconica; 29*tr* Corbis/Maxine Hall; 30*bl* Topfoto; 30–31*t* SPL/Christian Darkin; 31*tr* Getty/Imagebank; 31*bl* Alamy/Paul Rapson; 32–33*t* Alamy/Lisa Ryder; 32*bl* Getty/Hulton; 33*tl* Empics/AP; 33*tr* Topfoto; 33*b* Getty News/Andreas Rentz; 34*cr* Getty/Hulton; 34*bl* Rex Features; 34–35 Rex Features; 35*tr* SPL/Andrew Syred; 35*br* Corbis/Reuters; 36 Getty News/Andreas Rentz; 37 SPL/Gusto; 38–39 Corbis/ZUMA; 38*tl* Mary Evans Picture Library; 39*tl* Photolibrary.com; 39*br* Topfoto; 40–41 China Photos; 40*tl* Getty/Hulton; 40*c* Corbis/Sygma; 41*tl* Corbis/zefa; 42–43 Getty/NGS; 42*cl* Ullstein Bild; 42–43*b* Getty/NGS; 43*cr* Topfoto; 43*br* Alamy/Alan Spencer; 44–45 SPL/Victor Habbick Visions; 44*cl* SPL/U.S. Air Force; 44*br* Topfoto; 45*tr* Topfoto; 45*br* Topfoto; 46*tl* SPL/Novosti; 46*b* SPL/NASA; 47*t* Rex Features; 47*b* NASA; 48 Photolibrary.com; 49 SPL/Gusto; 50–51 Getty/Imagebank; 50*tl* Mary Evans Picture Library; 51*tl* SPL/Pascal Goetgheluck; 51*br* Rex Features; 52*tl* Getty News/Joe Raedle; 52*tr* SPL/David Parker; 52*bl* SPL/Eye of Science; 53 SPL/Christian Darkin; 54–55*c* SPL/Eurelios; 54*bl* SPL/Russell Kightley; 55*tr* SPL/Roslin Institute/Eurelios; 55*c* Corbis/Karen Kasmauski; 55*cb* Alamy/Photofusion; 56*c* Photolibrary.com; 56*bl* Rex Features; 56–57*t* Rex Features; 57*cr* Still Pictures; 57*b* Photolibrary.com; 58 Rex Features; 59 Corbis/David Kadlubowski; 60 Corbis/Robert Harding; 61 SPL/Tek Image; 64 Getty/Hulton